T0158907

VOICES
from the
SHORE

Songs of Truth, Happiness, Hope and Despair

CECILE A. JARRETT

iUniverse, Inc.
New York   Bloomington

iUniverse books may be ordered through booksellers or by contacting:

iUniverse
1663 Liberty Drive
Bloomington, IN 47403
www.iuniverse.com
1-800-Authors (1-800-288-4677)

ISBN: 978-1-4502-1364-6 (sc)
ISBN: 978-1-4502-1365-3 (ebook)

Printed in the United States of America

iUniverse rev. date: 08/09/2010

DEDICATION

This work is dedicated to all the members of my immediate family: Norman, my husband and all our children and grandchildren; and to the members of my extended family in Jamaica, around the Caribbean and the North American Diaspora.

ACKNOWLEDGMENT

The opinions and suggestions of many of my past and present colleagues and the feedback from several critics have been incorporated in this anthology. Deserving special mention for their contribution on how the work could be improved to create a universal appeal are:

Madam Jean Small — retired lecturer of French, University of the West Indies, who critiqued the anthology before I submitted it for publication

Professor Edward Kamau Brathwaite — poet, historian and philosopher, who mentored and encouraged me when I embarked on this journey in the mid-seventies

Dr. Winsome Gordon — former lecturer, College of Arts, Science and Technology, now the University of Technology, who inspired me to continue with the craft when I thought of giving up

Mr. Vivian Crawford, Executive Chairman — Institute of Jamaica, for encouraging me to publish the work without delay

Professor Verene Shepherd — historian, University of the West Indies, who reviewed the final version of my work and provided me honest, critical feedback

Ann-Marie Jarrett — my daughter for her invaluable help in editing the draft and for teaching me advanced word processing techniques

Mr. Michael Reckord — former colleague, critic, author and lecturer for the time he invested in scanning the print-ready draft and providing feedback

The IUniverse team, whom I found to be professionally honest, encouraging and helpful

Finally, the contribution of the many women and few men across

Jamaica and the Caribbean, who shared their agony, disappointments, fortitude in overcoming adversities; their sorrows, joys and successes, provided me abundant and invaluable themes and content for the work.

ORIKI

Praise the mountains
Praise the hills
Praise the valleys
Praise the heat and the chills
Praise the forests; praise the seas
Praise the people
Birds and bees
Everything with breath
Help me praise more than all of these

Cecile A. Jarrett

THE SAD GOODBYE

With regret
I take this final gaze
the final clump moved
weeks creep slowly
into months
months crawl to the finish line
the ghastly, mechanical monster
gnawed out another wound
in the range

Must all the hills
be flattened to please
a few escapees?
The soothing puffs of wind
from our blue range
energy-giving music from the birds;
sweet smell of flowers
carried down
to open hearts
gradually disappear

Can those
clustered, concrete mansions
replace the bosom of the hill?
glass glares in daylight
piercing the straining eye
no natural night light
just bulbs ... electric bulbs

Gone too
the thread of smoke
festooning the sky,
denying waiting spirits
the daily trip
forcing out my sigh
and goodbye
to another precious piece of Blue Mountain Range

LOOK OUT

There you lie below me
Innocent of your wealth
Quiet as a sleeping child
On this Friday afternoon

The haze rolls gently down
Caressing your towering structures
The Hilton, Adventure Inn
Mutual Life, those in the
Kingston Mall ...
Breathtaking
From up here

From here
You belie
The gulf between Trench Town
Jones Town, Lizard Lane
Beverley Hills
Cherry Gardens and Barbican

Your fame for the slaughter
The lethal blow
Is forgiven
By these greens and greys and blues
Your centre folds
Below this prodigality
Of tropical greens

Topped with misty blue
Mesmerized and brought closer
To a love of larger things;
My being rises to consume
Or be consumed.

Another glance
It ... meets the sea
I'm lost in tranquillity
My own senses numb
I step forward on a rock
Look out!
Beyond this panorama
And this trance
Lies my city festering
Cries my city ... Who is listening?

THE SUMMIT

Absorbed in your beauty
Your quietness
     Your balm
Compelled by this scenery
The smell
     The shyness
     Of the afternoon
Inspired by these heights
These depths
     These plains—barely visible from here

From the foot of the hills
Your height is disquieting
You look unconquerable, but inviting
Luring travellers to your charm

The climb is hardly felt
Coniferous height, unbelievable from below
Meet and greet you as you go
Losing you in acres,
Oozing tales of stolen felled pine

Above, clusters of emerald
Await
Another climb brings you closer
To deceptive folds
And the meanness of the test
To conquer ... Mother Blue

Further up
The challenge isn't easy
Temperature falls with each upward step
Wayside streams drench the earth and
For the moment, you forget

Absorbed in nature's philanthropy
    Eyes look inward
    To this peace, this thought;
    Behind all this
    Lies something all powerful
    Something ordered
    Something real
    Something large, vast, expansive
    Something my humbled heart leaps to grasp
    I stooped
    I worshipped
    And reached the summit!

MIDNIGHT IN THE VALLEY

Fast asleep!
All four
What strange dreams
Disturb those minds?

Why
Can't I sleep?
Why
Does this new house creak?

Valiums—he
Takes a ten
Now and then
Said he couldn't
Be here ... with us
Why do the stray dogs
Bark?

I can't sleep
REM, please come near me
My teenage son's in by now
Glad I'm not there
To hear
The blasphemy
Between them

All is quiet
So peaceful, so still
The stage is set
I'll drench my thoughts with images
Of natural things

One moonbeam
Strayed through the window
It lingered on the floor
The trees
Cast a shadow
It reflected in the mirror
The wind got stronger
And quarrelled
With the roof
M-o-o-n-b-e-a-m
T-r-e-e-s w-i-n-d
S-h-a-d-o-w s-h-a-d-o-w-w-w-w-w-w o-h ...

DISCOVERY

Content Gap
Is not a gap
It's a basin
Blue Mountain's fertile basin

Content Gap
Is on the hill
But it's a valley
Blue Mountain's fertile valley

Content Gap
Is untamed
But a farming village
Blue Mountain's fertile farming village

Content Gap
Is many experiences
But they are cryptic
Blue Mountain's cryptic topography

Content Gap
Whatever you are
You're captivating.
Blue Mountain's captivating, peaceful, rugged community

TIME

No clock
To tick the time
Wireless
Left behind
TV?
Leisure for the urban mind
Newspapers—no
Shirk to think
Of what's happening below
My flight is from the decay

From that life
That refuses to pause
To see
The rising sun
Creating daily time
Moving
Testing
The senses

Semi-circular white
A prism of rays
Blinding the naked eye
A prism disobeying
Its
Own laws
Blackens the eye

Half-open; half-watering
A rainbow appears
Other suns dance before
Earth's brightest star

Eyes weaken
Can't withstand the blast
To see; to feel
The sun creating time

Climbing
By measured degree
The arc glows
Bringing white
Life to this valley
Calling Nature to celebrate

DUNN'S RIVER FALLS

Veiled
In lace-like splendour
Flowing
In flaxen form
Candy
In preparation
Glass
Being blown
Gently
Caressing boulders
Cascading past the green
Soothing every lock of hair
Allaying human fear
And this pool
Below your bellowing wall
Heightens your charm
Triggers my alarm

SEA SPRAY

Caribbean Blue
Caress these souls anew
Caribbean Blue
Across the salt they
Sailed to you

Meet them
Greet them
Embrace them
In your warmth
Caribbean Blue

Strangers—sometimes many
Sometimes few
Some seeking
Some shrieking
Some surrender
Some remember
Some choose to forget
Caribbean Blue

Your pebbles
Their treasure, danger, charm
Without any alarm
Told of no harm
Caribbean Blue

My challenge,
My history: present-past-and-future
My call
Caribbean Blue
Taste the salt
It's of the earth
Taste the salt
My land; my birth
Taste the salt
Hold the future in your hand.

THE SEA AND ME: PART I

You have always failed me
I don't know why
Your heaviness disturbs
And your ebbing haunts

Often times I look to you
Seeking inspiration, a line or two
Something about you discomfits
I can't get through

Your ceaseless, sensuous heaving
Swings the mood to mundane things
Pleasures to be derived
Perhaps a lustful fling

You seep into the bones
And through the body
Skilfully eluding the mind
What is it about your movement
I find so unkind?

Can't you be my mentor?
Can't you be my muse?
Can't you provide other images,
That leave me less confused?

The answer?
That I may not get
I'll keep on trying
In a more secluded spot maybe
Where there's only you and me
And this gentle wind

I'll listen to its whisper
I'll figure the mystery
I'll ignore the whim
I'll lift my mind beyond your blanket-like rolling
And this immediate urge

THE SEA AND ME: PART II

Now I know
You do not elude
You remind
Remind me of the past
You favoured the trade
Your waves brought them here
I'm not angry
Just wary

Sailing, sailing
Over waters blue
Captains embraced
The splendour
Of your tropic hue

Blacks
Below decks—chained
Stank—sighed—died
Dropped overboard;
Whites
Above deck-chained
Drank, feared, prayed
Cringed;
Died inside

Two worlds met
Cultures mis-
Interpreted
Superior; inferior;
Which is which?

A clash began
Only to continue
To today
In this secluded spot
This island plot
The legacy—this legacy man
Reincarnated mishap
And you
"big river without shores"
Roll on
Roaming our Caribbean archipelago
While
Our human treasure waiting
Lying on your floor
Not for us to explore
But to bring closure
And final rest
And final rest.

THE TIDES

Low tide
waves no longer troubled
but at rest
low tide
only the whisper in the wind
silence on the shore
voices soar and float
above lost fishermen
clinging to splinters of a boat
a bitter, salty tale to tell ...

high tide
business fine
cotton mills roll
steam's the latest thing
dockyards busy
"remodel this ship,
stretch lower deck
trade is good, lots of cargo
from far inside the *dark* continent
it's big you know"
... trinkets—more mirrors please
mirrors please the chiefs
more prized than guns
is the image you know; the image
seeing themselves in the marvel

mirror, mirror on the wall
mirror, mirror on the wall
who is the greediest of us all
who will rise; who will fall?
mothers bawling
village upside down
puberty rites postponed
brothers clashing … war and woe
lovers fear and tremble
no caresses
under the moon
storytellers absent; history hibernates
no drums
no dancing
no wedding feast
no weaving
no carving
no kente cloth;
only emptiness
only the mask
the smile
we got to wear
or be forever lost.

mirror, mirror on the wall
mirror, mirror on the wall
who is the strongest of us all?

who will rise; who will fall?
"leave the mask
no, we'll take them
got to wear them to the last"

low tide
ships won't move
"lighten the burden
choose the frail
ease them off
later in the dark"
"quaamie, dead
sidi, iki and oku, too
can't count
nuff a wi people gawn fi true."

low tide
prices turn ping-pong
markets drying up
sell them quick
for any ole dime

low tide
parting ways
is painful
low tide
arrival and beginning
low tide
mirrors crack

low tide
the struggle
is eternal
Destiny must be controlled
But Maas Big
Lost his grip
And Generation X slipped
Lost, absorbed forever—or struggling
To return

DE ISLAND IS MY MOTHER

Long, hard years she toil
Long, hard years she lay
    in the sun
Long, hard years she walk
    in the rain
She siddung pon de grung
Long, hard years
    and nothing to show for it
Nothing to count for it
Long, hard years
And now she lying on she back
    Flat
Flat like bammy presser
    Still
Still like pond water
Me mother lying pon she back
An' can't do nothing
An' can't give nothing
Me mother, she lying flat
On she back
And her pickney dem
    getting worse
What a curse!
All day long
Dem holla ... fahda
All day long dem wrenching ... hunga
All day long dem chantin ... Christ

But he dead 'pon Calvary Cross
Him rise up
And live too far

While
De rock getting hotter
An' de sun burning hotter
An' me muddah open up an crack
An' de pickney dem does bawl
An' her customers stop call!

Nobody to tease her
Nobody to bring her down
Cause mamma get older
And mamma is much colder
And is not de beloved anymore.

But we still join in and sing
    Jamaica, Jamaica
    Jamaica Land
    We love ...

THE POLITICS

of the

PEOPLE

CARIB'S NEW DIAMOND

The people did not cheer
The people did not sing
The people did not know
Their Tuesday morning
Would bring
A Jewel
That has a movement
Like a watch with a new spring
A newly formed Diamond
In a sleepy state
Waiting to dream
Or otherwise scheme
To create its own fate

For this New Jewel
Has a movement
A movement
That did surprise
Just before sunrise

Before dawn
And dawn must be the right time
To be born
And dawn must bless this new gem
With special favours
To make it glow
And guide a people

For eighteen years misguided
For eighteen years ill-used

Never shall the leader be
Joshua
Who stayed the sun
After three
What's to be done must be done
For all the world to see—
A New Jewel
Is gazed upon
To show whether it'll be blessed by the Son

Look! Joshua's sun's in stasis
Joshua's moon eclipsed
And Jewels must be careful
It is gazed upon;
Get to the start
Choose the right path
You're a *diamond*
At heart
For Carib has had many jewels
And many were diamonds too
Some got tarnished
Others vanished
Into bowels of the sea
They did not make it to the pages of history.

THE RED-RED ROSE

Hymen of rose blossoms
bursting into Red
tropic sun warms
yellow poui glows
singing with the rose
yellow poui
delicately yellow
      in white light
      fragile in the wind
      dancing as it calls

Hymen of rose blossoms
bursting into Red
in full bloom now
soon to be dead
hymen of red rose
unfolding to the sun
mindless of the worm
feeding below
      heedless of the monster
      that from it may grow
      Red or Black
      ready to attack

Tropic sun glows warmer
greens turn brown
brown earth breaks the caverns

in the hills
flames red and hot
fan the caverns and the rock
man flees Red heat
scorching the back–
tumults take the flight

See the caverns and the worm
my, how it grows!
dwarfing the Rose
a strange new sight
a monster bred
outright
to crush the Rose
unleashed
and hungry for more!
      tropic sun strikes hot
      scorching wounds already bare
      blisters burst into sores
      blocked-up pores
      putrefied Red rose … still
yellow poui's yellow
delicate in white light
dancing in the wind
heedless of man
and his brand new plight.

ROLEX TELLS GOOD TIME

The pendulum swings
It brings back things
To what they were before
Old Man Time
Stands at the door
Brings past time
Into being once more

Sixty-five grew famous
For what he did
Time himself miscalculating
Aided the undertaking
To the people gave foresight
Made some to see and despise
Oppression carefully crafted
Beyond our eastern shore

Post-Emancipation Slavery
In typical nineteenth-century colonial style

The colonial veneer
Really sneer
Blinding eyes to the blight
The machinery expanded
And some landed on foreign soil
The veneer unstripped
Completely ripped

By returnees from afar
With few from the fullness of the bar

Father Time was beckoned
And immediately reckoned
The right time for another
Pendulum swing
Without hesitation
He did his thing
Thirty-eight, upheavals,
Underpaid workers
Ignored colonial peace;
Forty-four, retrievals
A new day, new leaders
Our own came into being

Our own came into being
Our own decided
Our own began to own
The land
The ways
The sunny days
The privilege to abuse time
Father time—not called;
Refusing to be stalled
Stepped in
Made one big fling
Bringing us to Sixty-two
Now we are we

No veneer, no mask
Now we are we
Ready to complete the task
Now we are we
Not wearing a face over the heart
Now we are we
We'll plan—decide
Shape our destiny

Father Time checked in
And noted adults had decided
To move ahead of him
The price was big ...
Back-bending;
Gut wrenching
The straining
To meet the deal
Soaring, floating, growing smaller
The measure of the man ....
The Rolex on the hand
Mental Slavery
Twentieth-century Jamaican style

Father Time
Watched
Father Time saw
Leaders leading
Felt ignored
Got zealous

Decided to change the tide
He stepped aside
Blocked the door
Gazed a haunting gaze
On the clock ... and the Rolex hand

The pendulum swings again
Grabbed the economic chain
Looked hard and long
To see what was next
To reap this gain
From Economic Slavery
Wicked and wild
In twenty-first-century economic tsunami style

He sighed inside
And muttered slowly
"I'll try to shift the paradigm
But must grapple to accept the rhyme
The more the change
The more the same"

LOVE
POTION

A Jamaican Valentine

Happy Saint Valentine's
Day of joy and beauty
To you sweetheart
I pledge my life, my love, my duty
Happy Saint Valentine's
Day of wine, of song, of laughter
Today, tomorrow, ever after
Happy Saint Valentine's
Day of chocs and roses
And all that's nice
Happy Saint Valentine's Day, darling
You are the peas in my rice.

LOVE SONG

Standing up, sitting down,
Lying on the sand
Not a word said to her
 Not an outstretched hand
All is felt, all is known
 She must understand
This life, this is love
 This; your happiness
Why so far; he draws near
 Now arm in arm
Lips yearn; hearts burn
 He takes her hand
Muscles twitch; then relax
 What must be; will be
Shy hands freeze; he gets strong
 Daring to be her man
Tears run down; she's unsworn
Tears run down
 "I'll take you when I can."

THE PLAY

One o'clock—two
He unbuckled her shoe

Three o'clock—four
She leapt to the door

Five o'clock—six
He tried to get betwix'

Seven o'clock—eight
Why can't you be my mate?

Nine o'clock—ten
Dear God, why did you make men?

DAY'S END

On the day we met, my love
Heaven chanted; sent a cove
Earth danced—rhythmical and long
On the day we met my love
No worry about things that may go wrong
No—we laughed and loved
Our special love
That could only grow strong
    ... and when we share our dwelling
    No harm will prevail
    For me you'll be the perfect wife
    To you I'll give my full life
    For me there'll be no other
    So, my darling relax,
Don't bother ...
Why all this preaching;
Why so beseeching?
Is he really wooing?
Will this last; will it ruin?

UN-DONE

"A thing of beauty is a joy forever."
Did Endymion smile
When making love
To his maiden in the moon
High above?
Do our daughters cry for bitter loss?
The moon at the last quarter
Disappears—lost
Sure to rise again
Blessing fishermen
On lonely quays
Did the namer of the quarter
Mean a *quarter* to be tossed?

A tossed coin
Can't be treasured
Only for a purpose, measured
Staying only for a time
Gone and lost forever.

The mind—curses in the void
Searches past and pleasant memories
Turns once
Once again turns
To ponder, to question how, how could it be?
Moved and far from reality.

Dreading the drumming pain that questions again:
>Do they sit and laugh as we did
>Have I tossed my coin that far
>Was it in my star
>To lose and keep on losing?
>Why did we become strangers
>Failing to see the other's heart
>Strangers—waiting to depart?

Wasn't it "a thing of beauty?"
He observed it in an urn
I couldn't before my turn
So I sit
So I ponder
Why couldn't we last, last, forever?
>*Kingston Mall*
>*Has buildings tall*
>*Some with murals on the wall*
>*Kay was plain*
>*Bases lain*
>*Reggae's dub*
>*Dub's reggae*
>*Marley's gone away*
>*Today*
>*Some won't know*
>*What to say*
>*Some won't see the games I play*
>*But Reggae's dub and*
>*Dub's reggae*

Catch a line
If you may ...
"Catch a falling star
And put it in your pocket
Save it for a rainy day
Save it for a rainy day."
Why does my mind not stay?

WHY SO?

All is still
All is calm
Not a trace
Of the storm
Birds are free
But not me-
You locked the door
And took the key
The key is gone
I'm still here
I see things
Far and near
I see peace
(It is passing understanding)
Another glance
I see new romance
The key is on the floor
You locked the door
But dropped the key

BON VOYAGE

Divested of her virginity
Spring gives birth
To a green world
Choruses
Greet the dawn
Man lingers in bed to yawn
Another to life
April showers
Her showers in March
And winter days followed
Fast on spring.

"Her Winter"
Came in spring
Days grow shorter
In spring
Sending her lover
To a distant land
Leaving her to ponder
Leaving her to wonder
Are they
No more than
Strangers at a door?

The key
Turns once
Once again turns
Up he goes
Down he goes
Landed at another door
Who will take over
Now?

The key turns …
And keeps on turning
Life must go on

STAR GAZING

I sat on my balcony
I gazed at the sky
A long, steady sky gaze
I saw a star
One single star
I gazed at the single star
It shifted
Left, right, left
It hid
Behind the cloud
It came back
In front of the cloud
Shifting—always shifting
From my gaze
The tail appeared
Disappeared again
My single shifting star
Steadied itself and gazed right back at me

DANCING

on the

EDGE

MY GRAIN

The fork-pricked earth
Yielded
Another birth
Reaching
From the depth
Sticking, stiffening, suffocating
Clutching, tightening the cord
An arch-backed cat
A hungry octopus
Tentacles of unending growth
A crisp new coin
Tossed at noon
Blinding
Makes the skull
A dizzy maze
A flash of lightning
Metallic
Red hot
Scorching, parching the skin
Another flash of lightning
White, white the light glows
The sense shows red, green, black night
In broad daylight
Black—the noon, black—the room, black as the tomb ...
And silent

My grain *is* pain
Eyes sink deep, eyes can't sleep, eyes must keep
The watch tonight
My grain is pain, migraine is fright.

ROLLING CALF

De nite was cold
De place was dahk
All de dawg dem
Staht to bahk
De place get col'
It staht to roll
From down de lane

Mi bredda ketch im fraid
Mi run to him aid
Him insist
    Dat im hear it
    Yuh hear i'
    Yuh hear i'
    Yuh nuh hear i'?

Mi sista cough
Mi bus out a laugh
Him run to har
    It nuh far
    It nuh far
Him eye suh bright
It light up de night
Fire eena im mout!
Mi bredda staht to shout:
    Im a come
    Im a come
    Si him roun' de corner!

De nite was dahk
Mi sista still a cough
Tryin' to get im off
Har neck
Mi stay far and laugh
Mi laugh
Mi laugh
Mi laugh
Mi bus out another big laugh
Only mi bredda one
Si de rolling calf!!!

METAMORPHOSIS

Good evening Miss Mary, glad you're here for tea
    Good evening my child, I'm here for tea and more
    From last week your brother resting on ma' mind
    How is your brother? It's still a miracle how *he* became
    something
Ah, Miss Mary; you know his story well
Why do you need to hear it all over again?
               My brother was dyslexic
But the family did not know
That word did not exist so long ago

His *was*
Was *saw*
His 2 was 5; his 3 and 8
Never reached his learning gate
And when it came to 6 and 9, his brain fell completely out of
line

              My brother was dyslexic
But we did not know
Can you imagine how he felt
When his teacher called his writing—*crab-toe!*

Daddy grew perplexed
His teachers real vexed
To have him in class and ridiculed him with labels a plenty:
Dunce bat, slow poke, class joke, big jerk

Such abhorrent terms!
I myself, got converted and in ignorant bliss-unclaimed him
Didn't know who he was after we entered the school gate
But secretly, I admired the fruits of his two right hands:
Colourful kites, stunning variegated toy trucks
Painstakingly made
Myriad wood carvings, leather works
Clay dolls with moveable parts ... and more
Much more from his busy hands, as you may recall, Miss Mary
You remember his first toy ship?

Often I grew sad and questioned the cocoon
Shrouding the mind of our family's youngest lad

Then came the break—a call from far across the sea
From Jamaica to Germany
To study some kind of mysterious ship mechanic poppy-show

My brother was dyslexic
That is what troubled his reading and gave him two right hands

In Germany
They tested and tested and tested our family *freak*
From eyes to toe
And declared him smart and ambidextrous
But recognized that he couldn't turn his letters and numbers
Into anything sensible

They tested and tested him again and again
And came to understand;
He was near-sighted (some myopic shindig)
Couldn't see from the back bench
Where Miss Dixon gave him
His life sentence
And kept him out of the way
Of the children who were there to learn
    My baby boomer brother was dyslexic
But back in the sixties who on earth could know?

Say what, Miss Mary?
Yes, he is reading now, but in foreign tongue
Yes, he speaks it too and dreams in it too
Yes, my dear Miss Mary
My brother was dyslexic
That is why he took so long to grow
N-o-o: he is not short; six-two and over
I don't mean grow in stature
I'm talking about learning; yes, that is the name they found for it
    And my brother was it … *dyslexic, near-sighted and*
    easily excited
But we did not know about it
Only his lingering learning pain

That's when Miss Mary drew real close, looked me in the eye;
Then whispered in my right ear:
    Tell me, Miss C
    I don't think I understand

How God could make your brother
Twice a man!
And how such a thing could affect his brain
And give him learning pain even with knowing
his prayers
For, said she …
He is not the only one I have heard about like that
As another fellow from back bush got a trip to
America
And turned green *tam* but couldn't get draft
For Afghanistan
Because he wasn't just one
But really two men in one man's body
And she continued with her brand of ignorance
Asking, pray tell
How is that word spell?
And many, many unkind things about dyslexia
And the curse that God placed
Upon my younger brother by giving him *lexic* parts
To impair his manhood

"Stop, Miss Mary!" I shouted
Please don't go that far; it has nothing to do with parts below
the bar
But with real slowness to fix his numbers and letters in his head
(Slack church-going woman with a son a reputable canon)

But back to my brother's story …
He became his father's joy and pride

Marine mechanic number one
Travelling all of God's ocean,
From South Africa to Iceland
California to Thailand,
Speaking many foreign tongues
Yes, there is hope for the hopeless, Miss Mary
Living hope

My dyslexic brother
Unchained his mind
Transformed his dream into a successful goal
Became Marine mechanic *par excellence*
And left us locked in this unbelief and perpetual trance

ROUND TRIP: CHAPTER I

Tricia went to England
That wasn't a bad thing
But shortly after arriving
Her troubles started to begin
      Tricia liked to talk
      And brag and sing
She bragged about her district
Where three parishes meet
She claimed a St. Ann link with Garvey
And Nesta Marley too
Said they blessed her with creativity
That makes her dance and sing
And fear no one; no thing

Sometimes she quoted philosophy
Saying, "This is straight from Garvey's throat,
My St. Ann family line"
At first English people
Thought it fine
But when she wouldn't stop talking to herself
Co-workers on the factory floor
Decided not to take it any more

They began to note
They began to write
They even invite
A shrink onto the floor

To hear her out
And chat, she did
About her St. Catherine heritage
Yelling, "I descend from Rodney
His statue in my capital"
She said,
"I am in England
To conquer this country
As Rodney did mine
A couple centuries ago"

She bragged that she couldn't only sing and dance
But also jump and prance
And take many a chance
By escaping through closed windows
And strong Jamaican burglar bars
Fly down a hill
Like Devil's Race Course
Faster than a bird
Any time of day or night

She talked some more
On the factory floor
And people branded her
"Crazy"

That's when, feeling fine as a daisy,
Tricia cleared her throat
Opened up her mouth

And belched out a
Dinky-mini tune
Teased with a strange gyration
She said Tackie taught her
Late one afternoon
She spoke with pride
"He is the father of my St. Mary side
A local warrior bred
Still living in this head
Dressed in banana leaf and all
Trying to get many
English girls to fall
In love with this strong African man"

The psychiatrist sat back
He wrote
Not a single word he spoke
And all this time
Tricia kept on talking
Tricia kept on boasting
About her lineage and district
Where three parishes meet in one
The topography that sent many people to live
In her head

At last the psychiatrist spoke
Tricia laughed saying, "this is a big joke"
When he asked unmentionable things about her past
Tricia stood

Tricia sang
Tricia mused ...

    The only madness I was exposed to
    Was in a church
    Madda Power's Pocomania Church
    Tell me sah
    Yuh think one visit
    Could do dis warrior harm?
He really set off her alarm
And she decide to carry on
Addressing Garvey first
"Yuh si dis Maas Mosiah
Dem seh me out a me mind
Don't yuh think it's
Very, very sad
To call a strong, sober warrior
Like me—mad?"
She turned next to Robert Nesta
And shouted, "*Bob*,
Dem treating me like a gong
I need your redemption song
Dis is tuff
It is mental slavery!"
She grabbed Tackie, literally
And ask him to come to her aid
To start a modern-day rebellion
'Pon the psychiatrist and the host of other man
Asking her fool-fool question
'Bout mental sickness

And the many places she came from
She pleaded next with Rodney
Telling him how his
Stature strong
And how she need him sinews
To deal with this modern English man!

The psychiatrist sat back
And listened very well
He told her the voices were not different people
From her geography
But different parts of her personality
He told her it's a thing with most Jamaicans
Even those from a single parish
And that for one reason or another
Many Jamaicans refuse to bother
With being one somebody
But a whole lot of people instead
Under one head
He ordered medication
And she swallowed pills with glee
For she no longer wanted to be three
Or any bigger crowd
Only one, single, deggeh, woman
That everybody could understan'

Tricia trek back
From England
And people hole dem breath

Some even start to fret
For de district shad
Had a sober set
De news spread all about
Dat Tricia learn how to hole har mout
And that in fact she was no longer many
But one, single, deggeh, woman
A wonder for all to hear
A wonder for all to see
A well-behaved woman
In her returned resident town—Jubilee
From where she'd take an occasional drive
To smile and talk
To Jamaica's latest wonder—
The bigger-than-life statue in Emancipation Park

ROUND TRIP: CHAPTER II

You remember
Tricia, Miss Patricia
The senior returned resident
Yes she, the *sane* lady
Forget to take her pills
For a whole long month
And got a long lost lunar call
The beginning of her second *ball*

Remember how she take
A trip to Kingston
Every last Tuesday
To visit a certain park
Well this time was different
Cause she went with vengeance
In her heart
For a certain woman

Tricia take a cab
That dropped her at the park
And she waited there
Till it was dark

Then she step up
To the statue
And staht to cuss ...
            Yuh si yuh concrete woman

A want yuh fe lef mi man
Move from in front uv a him
Give other people yuh space
A nuh yuh one
Want fi si him handsome face
If yuh nuh lef him
Uv yuh own accord
Mi wi haffi organize
To take yuh from this yard
So him can emancipate
Look at the handsome fella
Look how him strong
And big and long
Den she start to muse
She even get confuse
And whispered to herself:
Mi read how man look on statue
And it come to life
An' how Pinocchio turn bwoy
From wood carved with a knife
Why mek mi can touch yuh
And raise up yuh life
After all, mi would like to be yuh wife
An' though mi fertile years
Are ova
Mi can be like Sarah,
Or Elizabeth,
Or Samson mother
And produce as much as seven seeds

Tricia checked her handbag
And found too many pills
She swallowed the extra
Then fell asleep
Right under the statue
So big, so strong, so free
She dreamt about her seven children
Triplets and quadruplets
Born on the seventh day
Of the seventh month
One year apart
To start this nation over
As people of goodwill
Who will stop shoot and kill
And show *One Love*
And make Marley-Robert Nesta
Coo like dove
And prove to Garvey-Maas Mosiah
That we can work
Under one God
And with one aim,
Create our destiny:

A land of prosperity.
      "Wake up, Miss Tricia"
      Called the taxi man
      "It's time to leave."

HIGH UP

Hail Idrin
I an' I is Ras Bas
Hail again
I an I in control
Will take dis iron bird from here
To dere
Don't worry bout
Cruising height
T'ings like visibility and speed
The cally weed
Dat all man need
Will guide dis show
I hope to safely
Lan'
In Kinston
The Rio Cobre
Or on Blue Mountain Peak
When we dun
Hail again
And welcome
Have an irie flight

I MAN CHANT

I an I chant
Selassie I
I an chant
Peace an love
I an I chant
That Babylan
Must go down one day
I an I tell de daughta
I an I tell de queen
I an I tell de yootman
Babylan must downpress no more

I an I must love Garvey
I an I must iletrate
I an I eat Ital
I an I share same fate
I an I a suffera
I an I a bawl
But I an I fine *Kulcha*
An Babylan staht to fall

Rasta check rich daughta
Rasta tek brown queen
Rasta sway Maas Big yoot
Rastaman gawn clear
Natty eena Babylan
Natty buy cris car

Natty fly eena iron bird
Natty Dread reach far

Few less thoughts 'bout Africa
Few less talk bout dere
But ...
Natty pass him CXC
him GCE
Nuff higher degree

Natty is now lecturer
At U-WEE

REVENGE

Red blood gush
Veins dilate
The warm sap flows again
Heartbeats dance
Pulsating to a crescendo
No longer strong but wounded

... and the wound,
Oval and widening
Deep and deepening
Pained from deep inside

A cut in the soul
Whispered the physician
Himself a man

He could see the real situation
He who has the will to power
The will to rule
The will to enslave
And as enslaver
Becomes himself, a slave
Becomes himself, a fool
And the tool of other fools
For *man is s/he*
Doctor, master, slave or free
Who will live

And learn by life
That the spear used to pierce
Another's heart
Will one day rip *his* own apart?

WOMAN

Callous hands
Baggy eyes
Feet tired
From crushing defeat
A mind confused, battered and bruised
Still she carries a clean heart
Deep within
Cocooning all the care
Her little ones need not win

Drooping cheeks
Liver lips
No front teeth
But she smiles
She smiles
Smiles at insults and jeers
Smiles to her children's heart
Smiles that say,
"I care; I'll continue with my part"

Radar eyes
That see the questions in
Their growing minds
Eyes that scan
The depths
Of hidden hues and tones
Of thoughts—unutterable!

She knows
Learned and distant meanings
Though her book learning was eclipsed
When her chest started to peak
At admiring opposites
Who forcefully answered the call

She knows
She knows
God made her woman
God made her survivor
God made her lover
God made her patient
God made her strong
God made her good
His very own patent
Not just to prove
But to love!

SHE

Her golden voice
Floated above the wall
Her golden voice
Floated, filling the air with joy
She diminishes the nightingale
And rivals the late Maria C
Her mezzo soprano
So beatific; so free!
She sings to enjoy
Her song
And in her enjoyment
Soothes the burdened minds
Of others
I know her voice
But not her face
I know her voice
But not her name
I know that voice
Will gain her fame

ANALYSIS FOR THE PSYCHOLOGIST

Touch
My hands
They are mine
Run
Your fingers
Across my face
Allow them to trace
The outline;
Is it mine?

Put your ear
Close to my heart
Come on—don't be shy
Put your hands
Around my waist
Measure my embrace
Burst my bubble
Now examine what you see
Is it me?

Understand all that I mean
But did not say
Don't think about
What you think I thought about
The way

You think about me
Now that I did
Not say
What you think
I could always say
Is it me,
That you are talking with today?

Listen
To my voice
To my word choice
Follow
The course of my discourse
Do not guess
If this is me
Say, "yes"

HIGH NOON

It was the day
No—the other day
No, no only a day
Any day
The weather changed
A slow, silent, sad change
The weather changed
Replacing blue with grey

He kissed her early
That morning
And said, "Wait till noon"
She stood, she waited
She waited as she stood
The weather kept on
changing
She kept on waiting
Until noon

Noon came and lingered
Noon lingered for a while
Maizie kept on waiting
And in her wait
Began to smile
Her sun
Stuck up there
Her sun stuck

She didn't care

Noon, noon in a room
Bottled tight and kept
Noon, noon in a room
Maizie slept and slept
Noon, noon in a room
A room that sang
A single tune
"Wait till noon
I'll come again
At noon"

Noon stuck in her room
And she stayed on that tune

The weather kept on changing
Seasons came, seasons went
Maizie paid no rent
She decided *not* to sing.
She'd visit him

To her gate she stepped
She looked up high
Saw him there
In the sky
Fleeting, folding, falling away
Calling her to come

She looked up again
Then leapt up

He curled, he crawled
He came but went
The weather kept on changing
Mountains now of grey
The weather kept on changing
Clouds rolled away
She leapt before the car
At half-past three
They are together now
She and he

JAMAICAN MADONNA

This basket on my head
Feeds my children
Provides their daily bread
I rise each morning
Toil all day
And always
Am late for bed
I do not sew
I sometimes bake
I never get to take
A holiday
My children do not always understand
My children are ashamed of my hand
My children do not like the basket
They hate
When friends
Ask about it
My children—ragged, happy, lonely, carefree
My children—doctors, teachers
Lawyers, dread
Some alive
Some shot dead
Some show care
Some just utter "drop dead"
You and your basket on your head

I move on
Beyond the abuse of man
To my basket and God I cling
This, my legal thing
And though I am
No man's wife
I lead a wholesome and noble life

And with this basket
I'll win the strife

DAWN SERENADE

The party had just ended
He was in a rush
The party had just ended
Just a few too much
The party had just ended
Home was kneeling long and pious
"Lord bring him safely
Back to us"

Down the stairs
Tall and sleek
Snake-like now
The rhythm of his feet
Creeping, stealing
Carefully feeling the way
Through the dark

Out there waiting
Beautiful in the park
Ready to go
His vintage Skylark

The party had just ended
Home kept kneeling through the night
Time was courting daylight
Tall and stout
By the roundabout
With all its power out—
The utility pole

The Skylark was happy
As happy as she could be
He pushed her to full measure
Though he could hardly see
A hot prayer was ascending
Where is he
It's long past three?

The rap on the door was gentle
The officer spoke softly
The wailing wife screamed loudly
Lord of mercy
How can *this* be?
It's not his *time* to come to thee!

ANCESTRAL MOTHERS

Ancestral Mothers
Wisdom of our race
Powerful, mature, kind hearted, pregnant with zeal
Nanah, Nanah
Mummy, Mamma, Ma!

Ancestral Mothers
Ethereal Beauty
Spirits of fire
Hearts of gold
Nanah, Nanah
Mummy, Mamma, Ma!

Ancestral Mothers
Ancient strength
Burden-bearing
Courage-bent
Ever-caring
Promise-keeping
No relenting ...
Nanah, Nanah
Nanny
Mom, Mother, Mommy!

Ancestral Mothers plead
Yesterday, today, tomorrow
Through the pain
Through the toil and *that* occasional sorrow
Ancestral Mothers Lead
Leading Leaders
Liberators, Politicians, Poets
Priests, Lawyers, Doctors, Men
Ancestral Mothers
Mystical
Sublime
Enigmatic
Throughout time

Ancestral Mothers
Past, present, future beings
Eve, Eva, Evadne
May, Mary, Maria
Di, Dian, Diana
Liz, Liza, Elisabeth
Lou, Louise, Lousie
Ancestral Mothers all
One eternal Spirit
One living Soul!

FROM DARKNESS INTO LIGHT

Life is beauty
Life is truth
Life is the end of new things
The beginning of new ends
A bud in morning sunlight
A flower at noon
A green fruit turning ripe
The cycle of re-birth

A poem is beauty
A poem is truth
A poem is life
A poem is the beginning and the end
Deep within
It lies unknown
Painfully it gropes
To become its own

Now it's a thought
Now it's not—even there
Slowly it moves
One to prove

The pain begins
The words won't come
It hurts
Dilation begins
The pen's in hand
The green light flashes
Energy flows
Write it down
Words come slowly
Erase this one
Words have meaning
Write this down
A poem has meaning
Make it clear
For all to know
For all to share

ALPHA MALE

Big and bold
Head erect
Sturdy feet
A planted grip
That will not slip

Changing now
Pale green
Dappled brown
Think that
I'm not deserving of a crown?
Alpha, that's what I am
Omega, that's what you are
First and last
Not a neighbour; not a friend
Dare me?
You'll get the slam
The fury of my strength
First and dominant
That's who I am

Big and bold
Head erect
Can't you detect?
I'm here to protect!

Dare you stray inside
My turf; my boundary
I'll leave you in such a quandary
Don't believe me?
Come; see
The shards of those
Who've tried

BROTHER SHOW-OFF

His eyes peeped out from mounds of thick lids
Twice the normal size
His lips locked tight
Thrice the normal size
He was bitten; you can tell
Show-off was defeated ... again
Now by wasps
Show-off said: "I'll get that mango"
Number eleven by common name
Came in box number eleven from India to Jamaica
During days of colonial reign
"I'll dare the wasps
And the big saw-backed green lizard
And the fierce woodpecker by her nest;
I'll get that last number-eleven mango from them all
I'll conquer Mango Land"

Show-off climbed up and up and up
Show-off stretched out his right hand—a mile out
It coiled back in a flash
With its trophy
A nest of yellow wasps

Show-off zipped down the ancient mango tree
Nest of wasps in hand with
Half the six-legged population tattooing his face
Show-off reached the ground in seconds

Dashed to the river
Show-off crawled out of the river
Eyes blinded by their lids
Lips swollen thrice their size
Show-off laughed a heavy laugh
And gurgled
"I have won the bet; I have dared the creatures
I brought them down"
"And the mango?"
His sister geered ...
"See, it's left up there;
High up in the tree
Dangling tauntingly"

IN PRAISE OF POETS

Walcott, I admire the people in your Mythology
Gregorias, Simons and Anna
Derek, I am happy you deride Manoir
His type's been lurking round the region
Since our history began
Holy, you say is Rampanalgas
Blessed, I say, Blue Mountain Peak

I do not want to be cheeky
I do not wish to pretend
Your poignant words, island images and metaphors
I just adore

To enigmatic Eliot, TS
I look
A Cooking Egg
Is really something else
So many cells spent
Groping to fathom that *Waste Land*
You created
Musical rhythms, Indian dialect,
Madam S and your Hyacinth girl
Mr. J. Alfred P
That love song puzzles me
I, standing at the foot of the ladder
Thinking of heights attainable
But afraid to try

Miss Lou, you are up there too
Archetype, queen supreme
My Jamaican Chaucer
Advocate of our dialect
Of that International Dialect
You stand broad among men
Morris, Scott and Baugh
Calling new friends:
Lorna, Orlando, Muta
To come along
I will join the company later on.

I cannot vie with Frost
Whose woods are "lovely, dark and deep"
And who has many "promises to keep"
My miles are ever lengthening
And sometimes
It's difficult to sleep

My sleep is thronged with images
They float, they haunt
They even attack
Waxing and waning
Tearing and taunting
Making a ragdoll
Of me
Placing me at the bottom of the pile
For today

I still read on
Still push on
While I read the other masters of the craft
Coleridge, Browning
Other romantic guys
Wordsworth I admire
And often seek his hand
To guide me to this special land
And attainable height

But listen ...
It's Soyinka heeding Ogun's call
"The road is my concern," says he
I share his concern too
The road, though long for me
Has an end that I can see
I will take the journey
Painstakingly

THE KNOWLEDGE GRAIL

The conglomeration
Assemble for the quest
Knowledge has become a grail
Reams pile on reams
On tables, in waste baskets
Minds made
Minds vacillating
Others procrastinating
Weary grow the officials
Champions of the cause
Directors, warpers,
Enlighteners of the mind
the receptacle of pedantry
Third and fourth-hand learning
Prepared for modern-day
Galahads, Lancelots and Elaines
To carry on

STREET BOYS' CHRISTMAS LITANY

It comes without preparation
It comes without a care
It comes
They have nothing to share
It comes
Finds them there
It goes
Leaves them there
Their Christmas
Brings no joys
Brings no toys
No extra cash
No old or new friend
No new trend
No waiting in long line
No holiday pay
Nowhere else to stay
No church to go
No midnight film show
No parties, no hearties
No rich meats
Only the same sun
The hunger heat
The dry bun
Lots of make-belief

No relief
The God on high
Comes not nigh
A God in Church is even worse
He is not read about
No utterance from their mouth
Is not praised in written song
Have they done so much wrong?

Our God of love
Is placed above
Not as one that reaches out
    with our hands
And walks about
    with our feet
But blotted out
    with the loud shout
Of those who claim to know
What its all about
Who keeps him living ... up there
Not bringing Him to those
Right here
To those
Who may never know His good deeds
When choking in their garden
Chock-full of bitter weeds

THE TIME HAS COME

Eyes deep in skull
Penetrating stares
Darkening opaque
No object seen
Just a vacant stare
A lifetime captured in a stare

1938
Plagued with hunger
Strike, dis-ease

We met at that beginning
That long journey into
Muskets, guns,
Detention camps

Constitution
Framed, unframed and reframed
Still debating
In celebrations,
In-Dependence

Mid-sixties
Arrival
Hero—living
Not—dead
The only living one
To tell the tale
Paul gone—broke his neck
Gordon too,
Garvey, cousin followed
Nanny and Sam evoked
Gloom in celebration
Celebration's gloom
Rest
Rest at Bellancita
Rest my Piscean friend
Away from city heat and bustle
You await the call

Eyes no longer stare
Lips refuse to part
It's goodbye from a lion-heart
Living hero,
Now dead—
Celebrates beyond

TIMELESS VOICES: 1

What bangarang in de house
What a cass-cass outside
Why the hell yuh don't leave
O, is the Bible sey "Cleave"?
But yuh will haffi leave
Before de clock strike ten
Or yuh will understand
My peace that faileth understandin
    Another day of wrath my God
    Another day—an yuh deceive mi
    Another call to yuh my God
    Another call
    Yuh believe mi?
    I try to fine de peace my God
    I try and try fi true
    But when 'im drink de rum
    My God
    Calamity falls anew!

    Calamity on de pickney dem
    Calamity on wi all
    Calamity is all wi know
    That's why all a wi a bawl

Where is our peace in our valley?
Johnny couldn't take it
Him cut an turn a dread
Harry couldn't take it either
De police shoot him dead
Thamas jus turn fo'teen
Liza, twelve-an-a-half
An already all de neighbas a laugh big laugh
Thamas is mi new disgrace
Him only deh a' school
To run eena a race
Liza at twelve-an-a-half
Can only give joke and laugh

De last is on de way
An everyday mi pray and pray
An every time mi si de man
A caan believe
A suh in tan
But the good lord knows—mi is a prayer fan
An' de night de news reach de house
Calamity turn tranquillity
And I sang ... "Peace in the Valley"
Loud and long

TIMELESS VOICES: 2

You and your middle class morality
Will not get you far
You and your constant talk
About society
Will only send me to another bar
Whether you desire to, or not
I really think
You should quit this spot

       My heavenly Father
       Why is my life such torture;
       Can't you hear my pleading?
       Can you assure me that you are leading
       Your dear child to victory?
       The children God—the children
       Babs was such a fine girl
       Such a future promise
       But I never believed her
       About the games
       He taught her to play in bed
       Such a lovely specimen
       To enter the viper's den
       Of go-go dancing and much worse
       What has befallen us is a curse
       And look at John
       At sixteen
       He won't be seen in another school

Fate has really given me the worst
Of everything
He now makes coke, his kit and kin
What a horrible thing
To see his young life wasted so
With apparently nowhere to go

My Lord!
Deliverance was nearer than I thought
And though I'll be lonely without him
From now on I'll only do your will
My life will not cease to be tranquil

TIMELESS VOICES: 3

I took a walk across the lane
And saw people in their shame
I struggled one day down the street
And from the houses poured defeat
"Something's wrong," I said
Something's wrong, I fled
Up the avenue
But found nothing new.

VICTORY

Victory is ...
Not the battle won
Not the song
Sung when day is done
Not the medals, nor the colours given out;

Not the voices in glad shout
Not the pride welling up inside
So difficult to hide

Victory is ...
Fear outstripped
Hands tightly gripped
Caring deeply
The quiet midnight song
A tune
Few shudder to sing
Along with

Victory is,
Conquering
Self-defeat

WATER

Mystifying, destroying,
Saving, giving pleasure
Roughing up the roof
Gurgling round the bend
Roaring in the distance
Silent now my friend

Glistening in the sunshine
Gushing from the rock
Surging back to sea
Your power—a potent destroyer
Of young innocence

Fear death by water
The seer did not warn

Those children
Lost in pleasure
Collecting pebbly treasure,
Got encircled in your charm
Then grabbed by your arm

Surfeited, you retched
Spitting your ghastly fare ashore
Making light
Their mothers' labour
Cutting short
Their path
Water—salty; buoyant, water

In the church today
This Second Sunday after Easter
The generous font poured out holy water
Newborns received new birth
Salty, buoyant, holy water